Little Books

Lazy Lucy

Lazy Lucy

Chapter 4
Lesson 64: The Last Job of Y
Lexile® Measure: 620L

ISBN 978-1-62382-027-5

When Lucy was six years old, her daily chore was to tidy the hut. Now and then, she was lazy and did not do her duty.

When Lucy was lazy, her mother would say, "Lucy, the last man to get to the water drinks mud."

Lucy did not know what that could mean. So, she would just look at her tiny baby sister Daisy and say with a smile, "That is crazy."

One day, Lucy's mom came to her and said, "Lucy, you are ten years old now. We can rely on you daily to get water for the family. You must be on time. There will be many other people there who need water, too."

The first day was not easy. Lucy woke up before the sun rose. She looked at Daisy sleeping in her bed. "I envy her," said Lucy. "She gets to sleep. The watering hole is so far away, and I am so tired. I will get water after school." So, Lucy went back to sleep.

When Lucy got to the watering hole after school, the water looked like gravy.

Her mom smiled and said, "Lucy, I always tell you that the last man to get to the water drinks mud. I will not deny that you were greedy, but I know we can rely on you to do your duty from now on."

"Mom, you are not crazy after all. You are a very wise lady," said Lucy. From then on, Lucy was the first one at the watering hole each day.

The End

The End

Comprehension Questions

1. What was the problem in this story?
   a. There was a hole in the bucket.
   b. Lucy lived too far away from the watering hole.
   c. Lucy's family didn't have clean water because she was lazy.

2. When did Lucy get to the watering hole?
   a. after school
   b. at lunch time
   c. on Wednesday

3. Who is *greedy*?
   a. someone who feeds homeless people
   b. someone who won't share their crayons
   c. someone who helps clean up after a friend's party

4. Did Lucy feel bad about not getting to the watering hole?

   a. Yes

   b. No

5. In the story, why did Lucy envy Daisy?

   a. Because Daisy got to sleep in

   b. Because Daisy was a tiny baby

   c. Because Lucy wanted to be named Daisy

Skill Words

Lucy	duty	crazy	gravy
daily	tiny	rely	deny
tidy	baby	easy	greedy
lazy	Daisy	envy	lady

Most Common Words

a	for	not	to
after	from	now	too
all	get	of	up
and	have	old	very
are	her	on	was
at	I	one	water
back	in	other	we
be	is	our	went
because	just	people	were
before	know	said	what
but	like	say	when
came	look	she	who
can	looked	so	will
could	man	tell	with
day	many	that	would
did	me	the	years
do	mean	then	you
each	must	there	your
first	need	time	

Challenge Words

mother	school
sister	always
family	
far	